D1395202

#JOMO

# THE

# Joy OF

# MISSING OUT

#JOMO

THE JOY OF MISSING OUT

Copyright © Summersdale Publishers Ltd, 2019

An Hachette UK Company
www.hachette.co.uk

Summersdale Publishers Ltd
Part of Octopus Publishing Group Limited
Carmelite House
50 Victoria Embankment
LONDON
EC4Y 0DZ
UK
www.summersdale.com

Printed and bound in the Czech Republic

ISBN: 978-1-78685-793-4

Substantial discounts on bulk quantities of Summersdale books are available to corporations, professional associations and other organizations. For details contact general enquiries: telephone: +44 (0) 1243 771107 or email: enquiries@summersdale.com.

DEBBI MARCO

# THE Joy OF MISSING OUT

## #JOMO

summersdale

# *Contents*

# INTRODUCTION

### Choosing JOMO over FOMO

Have you ever experienced the fear of missing out (FOMO)? Sometimes it can be triggered by a photo on Instagram, maybe of bright white sand, turquoise seas and clear blue skies, along with a perfectly manicured hand holding an ice-cold cocktail. Why are *your* vacations never that good? Or perhaps the gnawing in your stomach is set off by a Snapchat of your closest friends partying on a Saturday night, while you stay in with a box set. If you have experienced FOMO, you're not alone. In fact, over 40 per cent of young people have admitted to it.

Luckily, there's a new kid in town — the joy of missing out, or JOMO. Believe it or not, you can have as much fun and feel even more fulfilled by shunning social events and spending time by yourself, doing what you truly want to do — and not what will look good on social media! In other words, it's time to start lavishing yourself with some serious self-care.

This book is a celebration of JOMO. It is packed with suggestions on solo activities, and how to listen to your inner voice and meet your own needs, regardless of what others are doing. Best of all, it will show you how to feel happy in your own company, be uplifted and realize that saying no to something can often be the greatest gift to yourself. So, what are you waiting for? Discover the joy of missing out and never feel FOMO again.

# Why FOMO Can Damage Your Mental Health

It's easy to dismiss your fears of missing out as silly, but they are actually a form of anxiety. Some experts believe they may be rooted in our ancestral need to stay in a pack in order to avoid being attacked by a wild animal or to keep near a source of warmth and food. Of course, getting eaten by a lion is highly unlikely in this day and age, but your desire to belong and stay with the group is still very real. Even if you've chosen to stay home instead of going to a party, being bombarded with images of what you "should" be doing can make you look at your own life and feel as though it's not enough.

**THE REASON WE STRUGGLE WITH INSECURITY IS BECAUSE WE COMPARE OUR BEHIND-THE-SCENES WITH EVERYONE ELSE'S HIGHLIGHT REEL.**

Steven Furtick

# CONNECT WITH YOURSELF

Often when we do something, it's because we feel we have to. For example, attending birthday drinks, going for a team pizza after work or for a family lunch. But what would you truly do if you weren't worried about missing out or what people might think of your absence? Take a moment to check in with how you really want to spend your time.

NEVER BE
AFRAID TO
SIT A WHILE
AND THINK.

Lorraine Hansberry

# WALK YOUR OWN PATH

A funny thing starts to happen when you put FOMO to one side and begin to think about what you really need to make yourself happy. You suddenly have a lot more time and freedom to do things that you really want. Instead of watching the latest reality TV show so you can join in the office chat at work the next day, you might choose to curl up with a good book.

If you're not out drinking until the wee small hours, you'll have lots more energy to wake up early and go for a walk or a run, cook a delicious breakfast or do something productive like clear out the junk from under your bed.

When you stop worrying about what you "should" be doing and start focusing on what you *want* to be doing, life will start to feel a lot more fulfilling and a lot less like you're always one step behind everyone else. You'll have more hours each day to dedicate to things you enjoy and as a result you'll feel calmer, healthier and happier.

#JOMO

# FEAR OF MISSING OUT IS THE ENEMY OF VALUING YOUR OWN TIME.

Andrew Yang

# LOOKING AFTER NUMBER ONE

The beauty of choosing JOMO is you're no longer chasing everyone else and doing what they want. A big part of this is learning to say "no" to people — but it's important to learn how to do this without leaving them hurt and upset. Using this two-letter word in the right way at the correct time is the key to empowering you to find your own path and to truly discover the joy of missing out. The power of no allows us more time for the essential self-care we need in our lives and this chapter offers some easy suggestions as to how JOMO can help us live a more contented life.

## PUT YOURSELF FIRST

When you agree to meet up with friends, work late or attend a party, often you are doing it because you feel it is the *right* thing to do. Or you are bound by your commitment to your job or your friendship and feel that saying no could have negative consequences.

But when you start to put yourself above others, you can say yes to all the things you want to do and know when you need to say no! This will ensure your energy levels and mood remain high and will help you live a more balanced life, because you won't feel forced into situations that don't work for you.

## CREATING WORK BOUNDARIES

Working nine to five as Dolly Parton sang is unfortunately a thing of the past. Who can honestly say they don't check their emails or answer calls out of work hours? If your boss emails you on the off-chance, with a question or task that needs to be completed, it's hard to say no even if you're at home.

To put a stop to this, activate your out-of-office with a clear message detailing your working hours before you pack up for the day. Then switch your mind off work until you're back in the office — and don't look at those emails either.

## Explaining JOMO to Your Friends

While meeting up with a group of your nearest and dearest should fill you with joy, some days you might not have the emotional energy to get you through an evening of socializing. These are the times you need to stay strong and turn down an invite. But that doesn't mean you have to upset people along the way. A short, firm explanation that you're taking some time for yourself and it's nothing personal should be enough to let your friends know you're not snubbing them or choosing to do something "better"!

# TIME IS PRECIOUS. WASTE IT WISELY.

K. Bromberg

# FAMILY BOUNDARIES

Family commitments can often hurdle any boundary we put in place. But that doesn't mean you should let your loved-ones steamroller you and ignore your needs.

Look at why you want to avoid certain situations. Is it the activity, an individual or the sheer number of people involved? An outright rejection can make someone feel unloved or neglected, so put an alternative plan in place. If you don't like the idea of a sit-down dinner with everyone, suggest to the family member who invited you if they'd like to go for a walk or coffee instead.

If you explain your feelings calmly to them, they will soon understand and respect your boundaries without you feeling guilty. And if you are worried about explaining to other family members why you never attend big get-togethers, ask that family member or someone else who is close to you to tell the others on your behalf.

# Simple Joys

Run a warm bath, add some luxurious oils or bubbles, light a candle and… relax. Let your mind empty. Don't think about work, relationships or where you *could* be instead. Simply focus on the warm water relaxing your muscles and your mind. If you're struggling to switch off your thoughts, pick up a good book or a magazine. Repeat as often as necessary.

# LOOK AHEAD

Memories of past mistakes, rotten relationships or work blunders can stop you feeling present in the moment and block you from moving forward. Let go of these feelings and emotions and free yourself from that fear of replicating them. By putting them in a box, you'll find yourself more focused on where you're heading. You'll start to feel an inner peace that means you won't be so concerned with pulling work all-nighters or dragging yourself out for dinner. You will feel more solid when you choose to stand still, rather than pushing yourself to do things you'd really rather not.

CREATE A LIFE THAT
FEELS GOOD ON THE
INSIDE, NOT JUST
ONE THAT LOOKS GOOD
ON THE OUTSIDE.

Anonymous

# Simple Joys

Go out for a walk with no destination in mind. See where your feet take you. Maybe you'll end up reminiscing in your old neighbourhood, or you'll find yourself in a coffee shop or the local park. Focus on the journey, not the destination.

## STRENGTH IN SOLITUDE

The ability to spend some time in your own company has been linked to a life of increased happiness, satisfaction and lower stress levels. When you spend time alone, you can address any problems you haven't had chance to contemplate — plus, you'll have more space to be creative and pay attention to your own needs.

# Simple Joys

Bake a cake. The act of following a recipe can help you to calm down and de-stress as you focus on the task in hand. This means you won't start worrying about what you might be missing out on. Plus, you've got something tasty to take into work the next day or enjoy with a cup of tea on a relaxed afternoon.

Nothing can be
accomplished
without solitude.

Pablo Picasso

# ... AND BREATHE

Filling your days and nights with social plans and work projects is a very simple but effective distraction. By stuffing yourself full, you don't have time to stop, feel and breathe. But it's important you do take time to pause and tune in to your physical and mental needs. It might be daunting at first, but self-care is the most important part of happiness. Block out some time in your diary to be by yourself. Listen to what your mind and body are telling you. It could be the need for sleep, healthy food or exercise. Just a day to yourself might be all that's required for you to be at your best again.

THERE ARE SOME
PLACES IN LIFE WHERE
YOU CAN ONLY GO
ALONE. EMBRACE
THE BEAUTY OF
YOUR SOLO JOURNEY.

Mandy Hale

# Tidy Your Space

The ultimate in self-care is ensuring the space around you makes you feel calm and positive. If you're going to reject offers of socializing to stay in, it's important your home feels like a comfortable place to be. And that's pretty hard if it's full of anxiety-causing DIY jobs.

Take time to clear your clutter, hang those pictures, fix the shelves and donate unwanted items to charity. It might feel like a chore but once it's done, you'll feel so much better about staying in. Make your living space cozy by investing in some blankets, cushions and a few pot plants — and it'll become part of your routine to water and care for them too.

**REMEMBER TO
TAKE CARE OF
YOURSELF. YOU
CAN'T POUR FROM
AN EMPTY CUP.**

Proverb

## Be Your Own Cheerleader

By spending time alone, you'll discover parts of yourself that may have gone unnoticed. Write down a list of ten things you really like about yourself. It could be you make a perfect cup of tea, or have a wicked sense of humour or great eyebrows. Don't be modest — go all out on your best traits. This will give you an instant self-esteem boost and leave you feeling good in your own company.

**THE LOVE AND ATTENTION YOU ALWAYS THOUGHT YOU WANTED FROM SOMEONE ELSE, IS THE LOVE AND ATTENTION YOU FIRST NEED TO GIVE TO YOURSELF.**

Bryant McGill

# Simple Joys

Head to a woodland, river or the seaside and be captivated by nature. Observe the colours, listen to the sounds of birds. Step quietly to see what wildlife you can spot. Breathe deeply and feel the air fill your lungs. Be present and in the moment.

## REACH OUT TO YOURSELF

Allowing yourself more me time means you need to feel happy in the skin you're in. There are plenty of ways to give yourself a bit of self-love. Write yourself a card with a positive message on and pop it on the fridge. This way you'll get a confidence boost every time you're in the kitchen. Alternatively, make a list of all your achievements throughout the week, however big or small, and read them back to yourself on Sunday evening, ready to start the next week with a spring in your step.

Take time to do
what makes your
soul happy.

Anonymous

## PAY ATTENTION TO YOUR FEELINGS

It's easy to dismiss our emotions as being "over-the-top" or unnecessary — but pay attention to them. They are very clear messages from your inner self and it's important to spend some time listening to them. Recognize your reactions and emotions surrounding experiences and ask yourself what they're trying to tell you. If you tune in to your feelings, you'll learn how to react to them and turn what could be a negative into a positive.

WHEN YOU RECOVER OR DISCOVER SOMETHING THAT NOURISHES YOUR SOUL AND BRINGS JOY, CARE ENOUGH ABOUT YOURSELF TO MAKE ROOM FOR IT IN YOUR LIFE.

Jean Shinoda Bolen

# MAKE TIME FOR MINDFULNESS

Mindfulness is the slowing down of an action and using all your senses to be aware of what you are doing. When you're eating, take the time to smell your food and look at the colours on your plate. Notice the texture and taste. How does this change as you begin to chew? Mindfulness can be applied to every aspect of life, whether you are out for a walk or sitting quietly in a chair. Try to breathe in through your nose and out through your mouth at a steady pace — count if it helps.

Simply taking the time to slow everything down for just ten minutes a day will calm any anxiety you are feeling around FOMO. If you're looking for some guidance download a mindfulness app or podcast that will talk you through some basic exercises. Soon you'll be practised enough to find the time to slow down for a few minutes each day.

# Simple Joys

Take some time out for a daydream. You may need some practice at this, so sit yourself in a quiet room and think back to a really happy place. It could be your childhood home, a deserted beach or a hike in the mountains. Remember how the sun felt on your skin, the smells and sounds around you, along with the happiness and contentment you felt.

BE
ABLE TO
BE ALONE.
LOSE NOT THE
ADVANTAGE OF
SOLITUDE, AND
THE SOCIETY OF
THYSELF.

Thomas Browne

# MEANINGFUL MEDITATION

You don't have to spend hours in silence to enjoy the benefits of meditation. Commit to ten minutes each day if you can. Find a quiet space and try to calm the chattering in your brain. Start by concentrating on your breathing. Take deep breaths in through your nose and out through your mouth. Breathe from your diaphragm, swelling your belly as you inhale. Some people find chanting a word can help. Acknowledge any thoughts that float into your head, thank them and then send them away again. Wear loose clothes and sit in a comfortable position, resting your hands loosely in your lap.

Like training your muscles, meditation will become easier and you will be able to last longer the more you practise. Your mind is used to being busy, so it will take a while to learn how to calm it. If you would like guidance, find an app to take you through meditation sessions and help you build them into your daily routine.

#JOMO

# Simple Joys

Learn how to give yourself a full body scan. How does each part of your body feel? Scan mentally up from your toes to your head. Acknowledge any tension or heaviness. Focus on the rhythm of your breathing. If it helps to count, breathe in through your nose for a count of four, hold for five and then release through your mouth for a count of six.

BE A LONER. THAT
GIVES YOU TIME TO
WONDER, TO SEARCH
FOR THE TRUTH. HAVE
HOLY CURIOSITY. MAKE
YOUR LIFE WORTH
LIVING.

Albert Einstein

# EXERCISE MINDFULLY

If you're looking for a way to focus on your self-care, mindful exercise can help slow you down so that you really focus on the connection between your body and mind. If a noisy spin class at the gym isn't for you, consider slowing things down with more mindful exercise such as t'ai chi, a martial art that focuses on arm movements and is often used to balance the mind, using the focus and calmness of the practice.

Yoga and Pilates are also good options as both focus on moving with the breath of the body, using slow precise movements. Find a class or stay at home and follow a YouTube video. Moving in a mindful way and noticing how each part of your body feels and moves will help you turn your focus inwards. It should leave you ready to face the rest of your day with self-awareness and connectivity. Perfect for a day spent embracing JOMO.

YOU'RE ALWAYS
WITH YOURSELF,
SO YOU MIGHT AS
WELL ENJOY
THE COMPANY.

Diane von Fürstenberg

# Simple Joys

Start a reflection journal. You don't have to write in it every day, but use it to get in touch with how you feel when you spend time alone. Do you feel recharged and productive? Or perhaps you're nervous at first. Write all your thoughts and feelings down and look back on it every so often to see how far you've come.

# TAKE A DUVET DAY

You don't need to be sneezing and coughing to have a day off work without any plans. Book a day's holiday or take some time off in lieu of overtime you've worked. Switch off your phone and don't check your emails (otherwise it doesn't count!) and do something totally different. If you want to spend the day in your pyjamas watching Netflix and ordering in food — do it! Maybe you'll choose to take a long walk or paint your bedroom. Whatever you decide, own the day and don't ever feel guilty. You'll find that when you return to work, you'll feel rejuvenated and your productivity levels will be sky high. Most importantly, you'll realize that the office can exist without you and an email left unanswered for a day won't end in disaster.

#JOMO

## CLOSE YOUR DOOR

When you're trying to seek out space you sometimes need a physical barrier between you and the outside world. Something as simple as shutting the door to your room will tell others that you are taking some time. It can also work as a visual prompt to allow your mind to switch off too.

Spending time alone in your own company reinforces your self-worth and is often the number-one way to replenish your resilience reserves.

Sam Owen

# FIND YOUR WEAKNESS

It's natural to shy away from what you see as your weaknesses. Often an over-reliance on other people or social media is used to mask these. But when you're spending time on your own, these weaknesses can rise to the surface. Instead of trying to ignore them, embrace them and really examine them. After all, once you understand what they are and where they come from you are halfway towards trying to fix them.

# Simple Joys

Sometimes returning to our childhood can be just the tonic for all our grown-up worries and anxieties. Sit on a swing and kick your legs high. The rhythmic up and down as you fly through the air will transport you back to a time of worry-free existence and your endorphins will soon be pumping through your body. You'll find trampolines have the same effect.

# THE JOYS OF SOLITUDE

For those who suffer from FOMO, spending time alone can be a struggle. Even a simple walk or ten minutes in a coffee shop needs to be accompanied by someone else, either in person or online. But there are joys to be found in your own company — you just have to be brave enough to spend some time alone and discover them. This chapter will teach you how to turn alone time into me time, showing you how to build up from a few hours of solitude to entire date nights with yourself or perhaps even a weekend away!

NEVER BE AFRAID
TO SPEND TIME IN
YOUR OWN COMPANY
GETTING TO KNOW
YOURSELF BETTER.
THAT'S WHERE TRUE
HAPPINESS
IS FOUND.

Anonymous

## TOUGH IT OUT

If you're used to constantly being around people and getting swept along with the crowd, spending time on your own can take some adjustment. At first it might feel slightly scary, but stick with it. Being happy in your own company is an important foundation for your mental health. Start slowly by spending just ten minutes in your own company without any distractions. Do the things you really enjoy and take time to be present in the moment.

# Simple Joys

Challenge yourself to a solo date. The cinema is a good option as once the lights go down and the film starts, you don't really need anyone to talk to. Plus, you get to choose which film you want, and you don't have to share your popcorn!

I THINK IT'S VERY
HEALTHY TO SPEND
TIME ALONE. YOU NEED
TO KNOW HOW TO BE
ALONE AND NOT
BE DEFINED BY
ANOTHER PERSON.

Olivia Wilde

# TABLE FOR ONE

As part of enjoying your own company, a big step to take is dining alone. It might seem scary at first, so take something for company such as a book, sketchpad or journal — taking your phone is cheating. It might feel as though everyone is looking at you, but actually plenty of people eat alone for many different reasons. You'll be able to savour your meal and eat at your own pace, and no one will try to steal your fries or split your dessert.

## GO FOR A WALK
## WITHOUT PLUGGING IN

Often going for a walk involves taking a phone call or listening to a podcast or music. Try stepping out tech-free. Alone with your thoughts, you will find yourself processing any worries or events that have been playing on your mind. You will also be more open to your environment, both the sounds and sights that surround you. Beauty can always be found in the world around you if you are open to it.

Knowing how to be solitary is central to the art of loving. When we can be alone, we can be with others without using them as a means of escape.

bell hooks

# Simple Joys

People-watching is an underrated pastime and can be so absorbing you won't notice time flying by. Choose a café or park bench and settle yourself down. If you're feeling conspicuous bring along a book or notepad. The idea is not to spy on people but just to watch them from afar, then you're free to imagine their lives, jobs, joys and sadnesses, however you wish. Perhaps something in their demeanour or their clothes will give you clues about what is going on in their lives and may even give you an insight into things going on in your own life.

# FLY AWAY

Heading off on vacation alone is not for everyone, but it can be the can be the ultimate JOMO experience. With no one else to worry about you can choose your destination freely, pack a single bag and just go. Perhaps you'll want to change your plans halfway through your trip — if so, just do it! Travelling alone opens you up to exciting opportunities to experience new things, absorb new sights and meet new people.

# IN SOLITUDE THE MIND GAINS STRENGTH AND LEARNS TO LEAN UPON ITSELF.

Laurence Sterne

## UP YOUR SKILL SET

One of the great things about spending time in your own company is that you can learn a new skill. Whether you choose to self-teach using a book or the internet or attend a class is up to you. It could be learning a new language or instrument, or something more practical like painting or knitting.

# FEEL THE FEAR

It's easy to mistake being alone for being lonely, but that is rarely the case when you are making the choice to be on your own for a small amount of time. Instead you will start to see who you are without being propped up by friends, family or a social event. You will start to hear your own voice clearly.

It's important to allow your inner voice to speak. You may have been ignoring it for a while, or the noise of your busy social life may have drowned it out. Either way, enjoy the opportunity to spend some time alone and get to know yourself again. The benefits will soon become clear. Whether you're heading to the cinema or simply flicking through Netflix, the choice is all yours. Go ahead, choose a cheesy romantic comedy to watch, order Chinese food and know that these few hours are completely your own.

#JOMO

# WHAT A LOVELY SURPRISE TO FINALLY DISCOVER HOW UNLONELY BEING ALONE CAN BE.

Ellen Burstyn

# Simple Joys

We can be so busy fitting in with other people's plans that we forget to prioritize our own. This weekend commit to visiting a museum or art gallery. Perhaps there's a special exhibition on or maybe you can just wander around looking at portraits or the history of dinosaurs. Spend as long as you like at each exhibit. By going solo you get to decide where your attention should be focused, and there will be no one to judge you if your favourite part is the gift shop at the end.

## RELEASE YOUR CREATIVITY

By saying no to others' demands on your time, you will find yourself with a good few extra hours in your week. Grab these with both hands and embark on an adventure of creativity. Maybe you've always wanted to take a life drawing class, write a novel or learn a musical instrument? It doesn't matter how good you are at these things, simply doing them is the achievement. If you don't want to attend a class, check out online for home tutorials.

# Simple Joys

Treat yourself to some new stationery. There's something about a shiny new notebook and pen that can put you in the mind for starting new projects. A fresh blank page can be just the motivation you need to write that all important to-do list.

**SOLITUDE IS WHERE I PLACE MY CHAOS TO REST AND AWAKEN MY INNER PEACE.**

Nikki Rowe

## TREAT YOURSELF

You don't have to break the bank, but if you've saved some money from turning down a social invite, why not invest that cash in yourself? A colourful bouquet of flowers, a cheery coffee mug or a snazzy new shirt will give you an extra lift and definitely help you feel the joy of missing out.

# TAKE SMALL STEPS

If you struggle to embrace JOMO,
set yourself a goal to spend a
certain amount of time alone
each week. It can be anything
from ten minutes to the whole day
(although you might need to build
up to that). Hopefully you'll start
to see a positive pattern being
created and time alone will soon
become a natural part of your life.

# Simple Joys

Create a mood board. This could be anything from how you want to redecorate your home to where you'd like to go travelling or simply a collection of things that make you happy. Cut out images from magazines and paint on the colours that bring you the most joy. Whenever you're feeling a bit low or lacking in focus, you can refer back to your board for some guidance and uplift.

DON'T SACRIFICE
YOURSELF TOO MUCH,
BECAUSE IF YOU
SACRIFICE TOO MUCH
THERE'S NOTHING
ELSE YOU CAN GIVE.

Karl Lagerfeld

## Problem-solving

Time on your own can help free your mind from those tricky situations that are flying round your head. It could be a difficult boss or a demanding friend. Whatever it is that's niggling at you, now you'll have the time to really consider the problem from all angles and come up with a balanced and thoughtful solution.

We need solitude, because when we're alone, we're free from obligations, we don't need to put on a show, and we can hear our own thoughts.

Tamim Ansary

# Simple Joys

Try rearranging your furniture for a quick psychological boost. There's something about moving your things around that can energize you and make you see things differently.

## SORT YOUR LIFE ADMIN

With only yourself for company, there's plenty of time to smooth off those edges that may be irritating you. Maybe your wardrobe ends up as more of a "floordrobe" or your sink seems to be filled with dirty dishes. Perhaps you never have time to do your filing, switch your gas and electricity bills for a cheaper option, or even set up a pension. While all these things may seem boring, once you've ticked them off your to-do list, you will definitely be giving yourself a high-five.

## MOVE YOUR BODY

You don't have to be an exercise fanatic to get up and start moving, as there's a class and sport for everyone. If you don't fancy a run or a bike ride, sign up for a pay-as-you-go gym class and try something new like Zumba or Pilates. If you prefer to exercise at home, follow an aerobics lesson or a yoga session from YouTube. If you're really averse to organized workouts, put on your favourite playlist and dance until you feel breathless and sweaty. Whatever you choose, exercise releases endorphins, which will boost your mood and energize you.

## Simple Joys

Read a non-fiction adventure book. A study found that when you simply read about someone else's awe-inspiring experience, you become more satisfied and less stressed. Who knows — it might even inspire you to embark on your own exciting adventure!

**NO PRICE IS TOO HIGH TO PAY FOR THE PRIVILEGE OF OWNING YOURSELF.**

Rudyard Kipling

# SOLO PRODUCTIVITY

There's a reason why you feel more productive when you work on your own. Research shows that brainstorming in groups generates far fewer ideas than when the same number of people work alone and pool their ideas at a later time. That's not to say you can't be a team player, but it's important to recognize that time spent on your own can generate some of your best ideas, which you can then take to share with your team.

## REST AND REPLENISH
## YOUR BRAIN

You wouldn't lift weights at the gym every day or run a marathon every week because you know your muscles need time to rest and regain their strength. In the same way, to constantly bombard yourself socially, booking in dinners or drinks every night of the week, will just wear you down. Take some time off seeing other people to regroup and rebalance. You'll be sharper and have more fun when you're with other people if you also spend some time relaxing on your own.

# Simple Joys

Pull on a pair of running shoes and head out for a jog. It doesn't matter how far you go or if you have to walk for most of it. Take a pair of headphones along if you feel more comfortable listening to music, or just take in the sounds around you. It will feel like an achievement however long you run for and by going solo, you can set the pace and choose a distance that suits you.

ALONE TIME IS WHEN
I DISTANCE MYSELF
FROM THE VOICES OF
THE WORLD, SO I CAN
HEAR MY OWN.

Oprah Winfrey

## DREAM BIG

When you're spending time on your own, there's no one to pull a disapproving face when you start a new project. So if you're determined to finish a 1,000-piece jigsaw puzzle or want to learn to ride a unicycle — just go for it. It's your life and you can choose how you spend it. Just make sure you follow through on your plans.

# BE PURPOSEFUL

Decide how you are going to spend your alone time in advance. If you want to go for a long walk, schedule it in. If you want to use your time to come up with some new creative ideas, sit down and make sure you do that. If your plan is to crawl under your duvet and watch a film, don't waste your time on YouTube. Spend your time with purpose and make sure it achieves the outcome you need.

## Simple Joys

Take your lunch break alone. It's all too easy to fall into step with others at work and follow the crowd. But take an hour to yourself. Choose what you eat and where you go. Instead of filling your time with chit-chat, go for a walk or sit in a park and read a book.

LOVE YOURSELF
ENOUGH TO SET
BOUNDARIES. YOUR
TIME AND ENERGY
ARE PRECIOUS.
YOU GET TO CHOOSE
HOW YOU USE IT.

Anna Taylor

## TRUST YOURSELF

Without others to please, you will be free to think for yourself. Not only will you learn to trust your own decisions, you'll understand the consequences that come with making them. And if you fall, you'll be able to pick yourself up and try again. Each time you make a choice — whether it turns out to be right or wrong — you'll feel stronger and braver, and you'll believe in yourself even more, without worrying about pleasing others.

Solitude is the
soul's holiday,
an opportunity
to stop doing for
others and to
surprise and delight
ourselves instead.

Katrina Kenison

# FIND THE BALANCE

While finding your JOMO often
involves saying no and staying
in when you'd previously be
heading out, make sure you
don't neglect the side of you that
needs other people. You still have
responsibilities — to your job,
your family, your friendships and
yourself. Ensure that you are filling
your life and keeping it balanced.

# A DIGITAL DETOX

With the average American adult spending around 11 hours a day staring at a screen and Brits not far behind, clocking up nine hours, it's safe to say you could probably do with cutting back on how much time you spend on electronic devices. Obviously if you use a computer for work or enjoy kicking back after a busy day by watching a film, that's understandable. But it becomes more toxic if your screen time induces feelings of FOMO, especially when you are on social media. This chapter will give you tips and tricks to switch off your screen and offers you some satisfying alternatives for how to spend your time instead.

## ENJOY YOUR OWN COMPANY

With social media comes the constant chatter of other people's voices. Whether it's what they're wearing, eating or drinking, too much information can overload us and make us feel exhausted. There's often no space for your own thoughts and feelings. By not checking in constantly with others, you'll find yourself more satisfied with your own choices — even if lunch is only a cheese sandwich.

## LOVE YOUR LIMITS

With most people owning a smartphone, it's all too easy to use it for everything, from shopping and messaging to catching up on news and social media. How often have you settled down in front of the TV to find yourself "double-screening" with your phone too? Set yourself some limits. Try not to switch your phone on until nine a.m. and make sure it's turned off after eight p.m. Putting a few boundaries in place will make you more aware of how and when you use your phone — and how good it feels when you don't.

## REMOVE THE APPS

If the temptation to log on to social media is too great, then remove the apps from your phone. If you have to log on through the main website, it will slow down your access and help you assess if it's really worth the effort, or if there's something better you could be doing with your time.

# THE BEST PARTS OF MY LIFE DON'T MAKE IT TO THE INTERNET.

Anonymous

# Simple Joys

Introduce "screen-free Sunday" to your life. Switch off your phone on Saturday night and when you wake up on Sunday, see how easy it is to live without it. Pop out and buy a paper instead of reading the news online. Make sure you have pre-arranged plans that don't involve last-minute texts, or simply spend time with your loved ones without being interrupted by WhatsApp notifications.

# OUT OF SIGHT, OUT OF MIND

It sounds quite simple but start to put your phone where you can't see it. If you're meeting a friend for coffee or sitting down to lunch, don't immediately put your phone on the table. Keep it hidden away in a bag or pocket to resist the temptation to check for messages. If you're on your own, read a book or people-watch to re-engage with the world around you.

## TOO MUCH TAGGING

If seeing a selfie with all your friends tagged stirs the rumbling of FOMO deep inside, take a moment to remind yourself there will be plenty of other occasions for you to be part of the crowd. Resolve not to log into social media until the next day and don't search for pictures of the event you didn't attend. Instead of looking at your phone, be really present in what you're doing right now, whether that's listening to music, reading a book or cooking dinner.

MY TIME WAS
BEING ERODED BY
A HUNDRED LITTLE
DISTRACTIONS EVERY
DAY. I WAS LITERALLY
CLICKING MY
LIFE AWAY.

A. N. Turner

## Simple Joys

Instead of documenting your day digitally, go old-school. Forget the Instagram stories, tweets and Facebook posts and instead sketch a silly picture of what you've been up, write a diary entry or send a letter or postcard to someone who'd usually read your posts.

THE MORE SOCIAL
MEDIA WE HAVE,
THE MORE WE THINK
WE'RE CONNECTING,
YET WE ARE REALLY
DISCONNECTING
FROM EACH OTHER.

JR

# SMOKE AND MIRRORS

With the daily bombardment of perfectly styled kitchens, lounges, breakfasts and beach bodies, it's easy to look at our own seemingly sagging, cluttered offerings and feel inadequate. However, it's important to remember that more often than not these images have been manipulated. That perfect shot of a new outfit will have taken hours of styling and a good few do-overs to get the picture just right, even if it does look like it's been snapped on the spur of the moment.

Don't forget: for every clutter-free breakfast table, there's a huge mound of tea-stained mugs, half-read magazines, cold toast and dying pot plants just out of shot. It's very rare that Instagrammers will reveal the truth about their lives, preferring to present the glossy surface over the duller reality. After all, everyone has their own ordinary and these influencers need to stand out from the crowd to attract advertisers and make money. So don't despair if you've got a sink full of dirty dishes — you can be sure most people have too. Everyone's human after all!

# Choose Wisely

Sometimes it's hard to stop checking someone's Instagram account — even if their perfect-looking life makes you feel bad about your own less glossy one. You might not even notice at the time but acknowledging when something or someone is having a negative effect on you is the first step to digital self-care. If you find yourself curiously addicted to a social media account and you are continually comparing yourself to them, then it might be time to unfollow them or hit the mute button. There will be plenty of negative people in your life who you can't avoid, so it's worth getting rid of the ones you can.

I don't get all that
social media stuff.
I've always got
other things I want
to do – odd jobs
around the house.
No one wants to
hear about that.

Karl Pilkington

# TURN IT OFF

If you're curious as to where you spend most of your time online, download an app to record how many times you look at your phone throughout the day and whether you're spending most of your time on Facebook, Instagram or Snapchat. Once you know, you can start weaning yourself off the most toxic sites or download an app to block your access at certain times.

# Simple Joys

Challenge yourself to do three things in person that you'd ordinarily do online. Perhaps it's a food shop, buying clothes or booking a cinema ticket. By connecting with another human being and creating a personal transaction, everyday tasks can become uplifting. Plus, it gets you out of the house.

# CLEAN SLEEP

We're not talking about fresh bed linen anda quick vacuum, although that could certainly contribute to a good night's sleep. Clean sleep means preparing yourself for bed mentally and physically to get the most out of your night.

One of the most effective ways of doing this is to stop using screens around 90 minutes before you go to sleep. Try not to have any technology in your bedroom at all and charge your devices in another room if possible.

Do not check your social media before you go to bed. Instead develop a bedtime routine that works for you and is screen-free.

Maybe it's a warm bath, with relaxing lavender oil, a cup of herbal tea and a good book. Cut down on alcohol and caffeine during the day and try some gentle yoga or stretching before bed.

If you can, regulate the time you go to sleep and the time you get up each day. This will help your body find its natural circadian rhythm — that's your built-in body clock and sleep/wake cycle.

However you choose to wind down before you sleep, make sure you give yourself plenty of time so your routine isn't hurried and you can drift off feeling relaxed.

#JOMO

# Simple Joys

Make staying in the new going out by slipping into a comfy pair of pyjamas and curling up on the sofa with a bowl of popcorn and your favourite box set. If your friends knew what you were up to, they'd be round in a flash.

## SLOWLY DOES IT

If you're used to feeling connected all the time, it could be trickier than you think to wean yourself off the comfort of always being contactable.

Try doing it in small doses. Take a walk without your phone or turn it off for ten minutes during the day. Allow yourself the freedom of not checking in all the time. You'll soon progress to longer periods of time and you won't feel as tied to your handset.

## HAPPY HOLIDAYS

A weekend break or week-long vacation is the perfect time to switch off your tech. It might not be practical to turn off your phone for the whole time, but make sure you log out of your email and all your social media sites for the duration of your trip. Now you're free to enjoy your getaway without trying to Instagram every moment and checking to see how many "likes" your posts have.

SO MUCH OF SOCIAL MEDIA
IS ABOUT APPROVAL,
GETTING LIKES, COMPARING
OUR LIVES TO OTHERS' —
MEANWHILE, CONFIDENCE
IS AN INSIDE JOB, IT'S
ABOUT HOW YOU FEEL
ABOUT YOURSELF
REGARDLESS
OF WHAT ANYONE ELSE
DOES OR THINKS.

Jen Sincero

## Simple Joys

If you've switched off from social media, find a connection in real life. Book yourself in for a massage. Research shows that even a 15-minute massage can release enough oxytocin and endorphins to keep the feel-good factor in your system for up to 48 hours.

## DON'T USE YOUR PHONE AS A SOCIAL CRUTCH

With a smartphone in your hand, you're never truly alone. If you've got a few minutes while waiting for a friend or a takeaway coffee, it's all too easy to grab your phone and start scrolling. Next time leave your phone tucked away and look around you. Take in your surroundings; notice the view from the window or the other people in the coffee shop with you. You'll feel much more connected with the world if you spend some time acknowledging what is going on around you.

## SLOW DOWN YOUR SHARING

It's understandable to want to share every element of your life on social media. Maybe it was your delicious breakfast or perhaps there was a beautiful sunrise on your commute to work. Take time to think about how much of your life you're putting out for public consumption — and how it might be affecting your daily decisions, from the clothes you wear to the food you eat and the places you go. Decide to spend a day without sharing — or if that's too much, choose only one thing to share each day. You'll find that when you're not worried about producing the perfect photo, you can fulfil your own needs, without considering anyone else.

# Simple Joys

If you're feeling the weight of life resting heavily on your shoulders, choose a cheesy pop song, turn it up loud and dance like no one is watching. Dancing has been proved to lift your mood and stop you feeling sluggish. For extra impact sing loudly while you dance!

IT'S SO FUNNY HOW
SOCIAL MEDIA WAS
JUST THIS FUN THING
AND NOW IT'S THIS
MONSTER THAT
CONSUMES SO
MANY MILLENNIAL LIVES.

Cazzie David

# LOOK UP

With your phone firmly in your
pocket, it's time to start looking
up. Commute without scrolling
and discover a whole new world.
Perhaps you'll spot a great piece of
graffiti art or an amazing window
box display. Maybe you'll see the
same person heading to work every
morning on a similar commute to
you. What's going on in the sky? Are
there moody storm clouds brewing
or is it a bright clear sunny day?
Connect with your surroundings
and you'll start to feel calmer
and more grounded in yourself.

## TELL FAMILY AND FRIENDS

To avoid anyone feeling snubbed or worried about where you are, let your friends and family know you plan to leave your phone at home for the day. Put an out-of-office on your email to save yourself worrying about missing an important work message too. Your loved ones will understand your need to step back and take some time for yourself. They might even be inspired to do the same thing.

**DO MORE THINGS THAT MAKE YOU FORGET TO LOOK AT YOUR PHONE.**

Anonymous

# Simple Joys

Head to a local market to buy fresh food to cook yourself a delicious meal. Notice the vibrant colours and smells of the fresh produce. Let yourself instinctively choose the foods you're drawn to. Often your body will tell you what it needs. It might be a basket of fresh fruit and vegetables or a freshly baked loaf of bread. Whatever it is, just go with it and enjoy it.

# SOCIABLE JOMO

Embracing the joy of missing out does not mean signing up to a life of solitude. It's all about finding the balance and discovering which people in your life give you a boost and make you feel good about yourself. It's also important to identify who makes you feel less than great and exacerbates your feelings of FOMO. Of course, there are those we cannot escape, such as family and colleagues, but some clever social tricks will soon mute their toxicity. Go ahead and hang out with your friends, but just make sure you're left feeling uplifted from the time you spend with them.

# THE JOY OF FRIENDS

The right friends can lift you up and restore your faith in yourself. Spending time with these people is never a drain because good friends will make you feel uplifted and happy. It's important to have these people in your life as they can also be good sounding boards for any worries you may have, and of course they will make you laugh until you cry. Such friends are very rare, so cherish them, as they will never judge you for being yourself.

## DITCH THE TOXICS

Toxic friends are tricky to identify. They can be lovely people who can be lots of fun, exciting and even very thoughtful. But they have one standout factor, which is their ability to make you feel terrible about yourself on occasion. This toxic behaviour can come in different forms, whether it's putting you down in front of others, saying upsetting things when you're alone or maybe not inviting you to a party. Whether they mean to do it or not is irrelevant; the fact they leave you hurting means you need to consider if you want this person in your life.

I don't see how you
can respect yourself
if you must look
in the hearts and
minds of others for
your happiness.

Hunter S. Thompson

# Simple Joys

If you're out in a group, it can be hard to get quality time with anyone and you can come away feeling as though you didn't really talk to a single person. If you suffer from FOMO, it can be tricky to concentrate on a single conversation as you're always aware of what's going on around you. Take the stress out of a social situation by going out with just one friend at a time. This way you can focus on each other without distraction.

# GIVE YOUR SOCIAL LIFE SOME ADDED VALUE

It's great to catch up with friends, but often a one-on-one chat can feel a bit intense and draining. Lighten the mood and make the most of your time by suggesting an activity you can do together.

If you like a bit of exercise, suggest meeting up for a walk or a run. Or if the weather is fine, explain you've got a gardening project you'd love their help with, or maybe they'd like some help painting a room. By working together on a joint project, you will create a more meaningful experience for both of you, making the time you spend together even more valuable and positive.

LET US BE GRATEFUL
TO PEOPLE WHO MAKE
US HAPPY; THEY ARE
THE CHARMING
GARDENERS
WHO MAKE OUR
SOULS BLOSSOM.

Marcel Proust

## MANAGE YOUR
## SOCIAL CALENDAR

It's great that you've identified the friends and family who build you up and make you feel happy — but don't overdo it. Acknowledge your limits and book in one or two social engagements a week, with plenty of JOMO time in between them. Otherwise you might find yourself falling into the trap of saying yes to everything, through obligation or fear of missing out, and you'll be back to square one.

1   GOING TO BED EARLY

2   NOT LEAVING MY HOUSE

3   NOT GOING TO A PARTY

MY CHILDHOOD
PUNISHMENTS
HAVE BECOME MY
ADULT GOALS.

Anonymous

# Simple Joys

Next time you meet up with your best friend, don't make any plans. Simply decide a date and time, then see where your mood takes you. You might enjoy an impromptu trip to the cinema or picking up last-minute tickets for a gig or trying out a new bar. This feeling of freedom will allow you both to connect and not worry about missing out on what others are doing.

## START A SOCIAL MEDIA BLACKOUT

Encourage your friends to join you on a social media blackout where you keep your fun times off Instagram and Facebook. Maybe a small group of you has gone away for a weekend or you've headed out for dinner. Whatever you spend your time doing, keep it to yourselves. This way you're spending time together just for the pure pleasure of it and you're protecting other people experiencing FOMO too.

## DEALING WITH COLLEAGUES

Work buddies can be the trickiest of all to deal with when you're trying to build a gentle world of JOMO. Because they're not your nearest and dearest you may not want to share with them your innermost feelings, but as you'll be spending most of your week with them, you also don't want to upset them if they ask you for a drink after work. Stay polite but vague to keep them onside; you're totally within your rights to politely refuse any unwanted invitations. Keep a ready set of excuses handy such as you're going to the gym, you have another engagement or even you're just too tired.

Lots of people want
to ride with you
in the limo, but
what you want is
someone who will
take the bus with
you when the limo
breaks down.

Oprah Winfrey

## CHOOSE JOMO TOGETHER

Chances are your closest buddies will have a similar temperament to you and will also be experiencing some social overload thanks to their own fear of missing out. Discuss your plans and tactics with them. Not only will it help them understand your new pattern of behaviour, but you might also inspire them to jump on board and start experiencing the joy of missing out.

# Simple Joys

If you're in the mood for a catch-up, book in a phone call or Skype session with a friend or family member you haven't seen for a while. It's a great way to spend some time together without having to even get out of your pyjamas.

FRIENDSHIP IS BORN AT
THAT MOMENT WHEN
ONE PERSON SAYS
TO ANOTHER, "WHAT!
YOU TOO? I
THOUGHT I WAS THE
ONLY ONE."

C. S. Lewis

# BE HONEST WITH YOUR FEELINGS

It's always best to be as open and honest as possible, when you're talking to friends, family or colleagues. You don't need to reveal all or be hurtful, but explain how you're really feeling, such as being overwhelmed with social events or needing some time on your own. It might really ring a bell with those you're confiding in and people can be more understanding than you realize.

## SEE THE VALUE IN MINGLING

If you're looking to socialize, chances are you don't have a shortage of people to spend time with. But not everyone has a life filled with friends and while social overload is not to be recommended, some people are genuinely lonely. Why not use your time to volunteer at a charity shop or community centre? Serving someone a cup of tea and cake and having a little chat will transform their day and will help you take stock of your own life.

## Simple Joys

Invite your friend round for dinner.
Make a fuss of them by cooking their
favourite food, lay the table nicely,
maybe even get some fresh flowers
or a pot plant for a decoration.
They'll feel cherished and you in turn
will feel buoyed by making someone
else happy.

## Plan a Special Day

It's hard to spend enough time with our siblings or parents. Book a date with your loved one and do something you'll both enjoy. Perhaps tickets to the theatre will tick the box, or a day out walking around a new town and treating yourselves to lunch. The important thing is not what you're doing, but that you're doing it together without the usual distractions of life.

**FRIENDSHIP CONSISTS IN FORGETTING WHAT ONE GIVES AND REMEMBERING WHAT ONE RECEIVES.**

Alexandre Dumas

# Simple Joys

Make a love list. Write down the names of all the people you love and who love you. Remember how cherished you are and consider what you can do to nurture these relationships. It doesn't matter how small the list is — in fact if it's too big you might want to reconsider some of the names on it. These people are your cheerleaders in life and you are theirs. Next time you've been invited out and you're not sure if you really want to go, mentally check this list — if they're not on it, you might choose to spend your time more wisely.

# CONCLUSION

JOMO can feel like an uphill battle when we are locked in a world that is constantly connected. This is even more reason for you to work hard at carving out some time for yourself. Once you start, you'll discover it's not as hard as you think and you'll appreciate how important it is. So, forget FOMO and enjoy your journey towards JOMO. It will be worth the effort you put in.

**BUSY IS A CHOICE. STRESS IS A CHOICE. JOY IS A CHOICE. YOU GET TO CHOOSE. CHOOSE WELL.**

Ann Voskamp

# THE JOY OF NO

#JONO

## THE JOY OF NO
### #JONO

£7.99
Hardback
ISBN: 978-1-78685-949-5

## EMBRACE THE JOY OF SAYING "NO"

In a world that favours "yes" it can take courage to say "no", but this simple word can set you free. With short tips and inspiring quotes, this little book will help you to harness the positive power of "no" for a happier, calmer and more joyful life.

# JUST
# BE
# YOU.

## JUST BE YOU

£6.99
Hardback
ISBN: 978-1-78685-233-5

### BE YOURSELF FOR YOURSELF.

Having a wobbly day, week or year? This little book of uplifting quotations and powerful affirmations will help you to realize you are the best person you could possibly be — you!

If you're interested in finding out more about our books, find us on Facebook at **Summersdale Publishers** and follow us on Twitter at **@Summersdale**.

# www.summersdale.com